WHAT REALLY HAPPENS TO YOU AFTER YOU DIE?

Find out, in this mind-blowing philosophical fable, hero's journey, and thoroughly weird cosmological fantasy by two-time Nebula Award-nominated author and award-winning artist Vera Nazarian.

Follow Norman J. Jones on his trip into the afterlife, and discover an amazing unclassifiable story that only begins in his moment of death.

COPYRIGHT PAGE

This book is a work of fiction. All characters, names, locations, and events portrayed in this book are fictional or used in an imaginary manner to entertain, and any resemblance to any real people, situations, or incidents is purely coincidental.

LIFE, INC.
A Cosmological Fable of the Afterlife
(A Novella)

Copyright © 2014 by Vera Nazarian

All Rights Reserved. No part of this work may be reproduced, distributed, stored on any media, shared, or transmitted in any form or by any means, electronic or mechanical or any other method, without the prior written permission of the copyright holder and publisher.

Cover Design by Vera Nazarian

Paperback Edition
ISBN-13: 978-1-60762-189-8 / ISBN-10: 1-60762-189-4

July 21, 2023
Rev. 07.21.2023

A Publication of
Norilana Books
P. O. Box 209
Highgate Center, VT 05459-0209
norilana.com
United States of America

LIFE, INC

A COSMOLOGICAL FABLE OF THE AFTERLIFE

VERA NAZARIAN

*To Giles S. Bignold
in all truth.*

LIFE, INC.
A COSMOLOGICAL FABLE OF THE AFTERLIFE

NINETY-ONE-YEAR-OLD NORMAN J. Jones drew in his last faint breath through withered lips and into decaying lungs. He closed his eyes for the last time, feeling the world and the vaguely concerned faces of loved ones slipping away. And he died.

Or maybe it was but a deep comatose sleep. Because after some cosmically immeasurable amount of time, he began to dream.

And then, woke up.

Norman J. Jones was as dead as falling snow, and as wide-awake as he could possibly be. And he stood at the Pearly Gates of Heaven or possibly, Hell.

Actually, it was neither. It was a misty whitish place, dreamlike, and without a horizon line or proper sky. Before him stretched a tall filigree-metal gate painted gleaming mother-of-pearl white, and beyond, a great fantastic looking building.

The building was a wild mixture of small colorful towers and turrets (reminiscent of a certain popular family amusement park the name of which he used to know, but which, at the moment, just barely escaped him), modern glass windows, Grecian columns and Roman porticoes, a gothic spire or two, several geodesic domes, a glass bubble-dome, brightly painted Dutch windmills that actually rotated, and, seen from the back, a giant neon-lit Ferris Wheel that turned slowly like the face of a clock. To top it all off, this incredible structure was garishly encrusted with brass rooster weather vanes that spun on needle steeples, modern streamlined wind-spire turbines, Oriental wind-chimes, many-armed Hindu god-figurines in sensual relief, paper lanterns, grape bunches of helium balloons, and on one side, the figurehead of an old Scandinavian sea-faring vessel. . . .

And incredible as it may seem, as Norman stared at it, the structure was in fact changing before his very eyes—walls replaced turrets, church spires sank, only to rise again as columns or Aztec pyramids, and everything, after a second or some other random temporal measure, became everything else.

There was a huge lit sign on the top of the highest gothic spire that read: LIFE, INC.

Norman stood staring. It was not quite what he'd expected. Not that he'd expected Biblical settings, or atheistic non-existence, or even an agnostic white light at the end of the tunnel. No, whatever he thought might come after the last expelled breath, would be something a bit more orderly and —dignified?

"This way, Mr. Jones! Please get in line."

Norman turned to look in the direction of the very normal voice, and he saw a woman dressed in a conservative gray business suit wave to him politely at the Gates that stood ajar. And then he saw the line.

The line, consisting of individuals standing single-file, wound like a snake back and forth in about seven loops in front of the Gates. Boundaries were roped off, and the whole thing was very reminiscent of the rides at the amusement park the name of which he had, like a peanut fragment, on the tip of his tongue. There was no scorching sun, however. And the end of the line, Norman saw, just simply appeared to fade into a mist, about fifty feet away.

His mind absolutely complacent, for one reason or another, so that he wasn't even registering surprise, Norman Jones obediently got in line. He simply walked to what he believed was the end, where the last person seemed to shimmer in the mist. And lo and behold, that indeed was the last person, and he simply slipped into place behind him.

The line moved fast. The people all seemed normal, but for some reason they all had the same drowsy look. They stared nowhere, absorbed in their own reveries. He too did not notice the others before and after him—maybe because none of them mattered, or because time was not moving normally here—he never noticed anything, only viewed the chameleon sight of the mutating structure before him. And then he was at the head of the line, facing the woman in a suit.

She smiled at him, fortyish, with distinctive gold-rimmed glasses, reminding him of someone. "Here's your ticket, Mr. Jones," she said warmly, "You may go in."

He stared at those glasses, wondering why would anyone need glasses, here, now. And he blurted: "Am I dead?"

"Mr. Jones," said the fortyish woman gently. "You are young."

And as though someone finally allowed him to note this fact, Jones looked at himself, and suddenly realized that his ninety-one-year-old body was no longer stooped, realized the sudden absence of arthritic pains, and realized there was a coat of dark, strong hair on his formerly bald head.

He also realized that he was in his pajamas.

Aware of his sudden self-consciousness, she smiled again, and urged him on. "Go on now. You look fine."

And then Norman Jones took his first step past the mother-of-pearl Gates, into . . .

THE BIG BANG!

He was the pregnant kernel of the Universe, and he Exploded.

And then there were flames, scorching with blue-white gaseous agony, and it was Hell.

After a timeless moment of adjustment to the white razor-agony, he realized that it was not physical. In fact, he did not feel a physical body at all —no arms, no legs, no torso—he was but a center of *presence*, a bud.

Another timeless moment later, he realized that the agony was something best likened to a retinal burn, as if he'd looked directly into the sun and lost all sensation in his optic nerve.

The original perception of agony gradually transformed. There was a strange cool clarity. He simply existed, with burning agonized senses. A cauterized open wound. . . . Retinal burn. . . . Auditory overload. . . . Seared tongue. . . . Carbon monoxide-filled lungs. . . .

And he began to *perceive*.

Norman lived a detailed clinical version of his life in the blink of an eye, and somehow knew everything he had ever done.

Not just knew—he was made clearly and systematically *aware* of every cause and effect relationship in which he had participated consciously or automatically, and therefore *knew* how everything about his existence affected everyone and everything else.

Every motion of his body shifting the air molecules around him. . . . Every step that his feet ever made. . . . Every expelled breath. . . . Every sound he made, and every spoken word.

Norman's self chronicled indiscriminately everything, all the way to the molecular level. Remembered and perceived it in a way where value judgments such as "good" or "bad," "right" or "wrong," did not apply.

And what was surprising—he also knew, on a molecular level, the physical, psychological, and emotional reactions of every entity he came in contact with, starting with the hurt his mother felt when his infant gums accidentally tortured a breast's nipple, all the way down to the simple pang of goodwill that he evoked during a second of casual warm eye contact with some woman on some street in some city, some time ago. . . .

And then came Judgment.

Norman Jones knew exactly what went "wrong" with his life, what went "right"—according to his own, and only his own personal *level* of understanding of wrong and right. For once, there were no self-defense mechanisms at work, no illusions, no fear, no bias, not even misguided love.

All was objective, and yet—it was perfectly subjective, personal, based on his own experience and comprehension of truth. For, there indeed was something that could be called Universal Truth, or a standard of being—Norman knew this now, felt it, sensed it.

It was simply the schema or pattern of things.

And knowing himself so objectively and at the same time subjectively—as uniquely as no other could ever know him—Norman evaluated himself. His self-determined life successes filled him with a buoyancy, like the stars, while his self-recognized short-comings sent him plummeting with a heavy weight of self-hate.

And when it was all over, and his senses still

burned, Norman realized what had been causing the ever-present sense of agony. It was simply the combined multi-sensual knowledge of *everything* that pertained to his self and the self's contact with the Universe that had been his former life.

For, during that instant only, he, a single entity, was given a readout of sensory data that the whole Universe contained.

And as soon as he knew it all, *understood* it—if only for that one instant—there came a kind of closing of intensity, a relief on the senses, and finally, cool nothingness—peace.

Purgatory was over.

NORMAN JONES FOUND himself standing inside a great hall of marble, done in an architectural style that combined post-modern, ancient Egyptian and Greek, and Byzantine influences.

Actually, he wasn't sure what the place really looked like, for it too was softly changing, things losing their fine edges the moment he looked away. It was simply that memory-thoughts of things he had once known and seen came to float on the surface of his mind, and he simply connected the images with the stylistic elements he saw all around. Or maybe, the thoughts were there first, and *then* he perceived what he remembered? That grand Doric column, for example, definitely looked like something he'd seen in an Ancient Greek history picture-book, and so it popped up, into sharper focus than before, only to recede as soon as he looked away.

There was no central source of illumination in the hall.

On second thought, maybe there was.

Norman stared up ahead, his mind moving slow and orderly—very much as it does when dreaming—and his eyes saw what he almost expected to see, created the reality before him.

On an elevated rounded dais, focused upon a throne, *existed* a *form* of light. The light was radiant, cascading into an auric shadow-outline to encompass the perimeter of the figure like a plastic bubble, or a violet corona on a solar eclipse. Actually, the whole thing made no sense from the scientific standpoint—why the light, where did it originate, why the figure. . . .

Norman stood and knew that he was looking at "God."

And so, dense and slow, he continued standing there, looking, and waiting for God knows what.

Apparently God didn't know what either, so the figure of light performed some fancy trick. The light fluctuated, pulsed, and then suddenly went out. In its place, electric ceiling lights flared on suddenly (yes, Norman realized only then, there really was a ceiling, and a very normal ceiling at that), and the figure of God lost its abstract light-blob kind of appearance.

God became a young, sharp-dressed businesswoman.

"If I *could* get tired, then you might say I *was* getting tired of waiting for you to make up your mind there, Norman, about the nature of *me*," she said. "So I just took on any old form you could dredge up from your memories. Sorry about this corporate shocker, but it was a matter of this, zombie Elvis, or your maternal aunt Bethany."

"I had no idea that Elvis is such a fundamental, deeply-rooted element of my subconscious," Norman began. "How strange. That's not even an icon of my generation. Or maybe it is—in any case, I'd expected it to be Frank Sinatra. Or, if you want to go with what the kids are playing these days, Kurt Cobain or Toupac Shakur. Maybe even Michael Jackson. But—"

"Precisely. I wouldn't understand it either, if I were you at this point. If it's any easier, call me Harry. Would a wand and round glasses help?"

"Thanks a lot for messing with my mind," Norman said. "In fact, it seems to me, *you're* all wrong. You're *trite*, condescending. If you were really God, a.k.a. *The Supreme Being*, you'd know better than to toy with me at a time like this. In fact, who's to say you're not the opposite, Satan—if there is such—trying to confuse me? Well?"

"You've got a point there," said the woman Harry. "I realize you're not sure you even believe in a God. And I promise we'll discuss Satan later. But for the moment, your perception of me—whoever I may be to you—is limited by your own mental state. And according to my own Rules, I can only work with what I've got."

"I see. Only I still think you're enjoying this more than you should. Why Harry?" Norman pressed. "Why not Beatrice or Darlene?"

"Why knot? Or is it, why nyet? Actually it's in order to shake-not-stir you up a bit, rid you of complacency. Like that ancient Egyptian deity Horus, whose human torso bears the head of a crocodile—or wait, is that Sobek?—and whose image makes you think. You've been through a lot up to this point—believe me, I really do *know*. And it's nothing against you that you may be feeling sick and tired, drowsy, remote. So, I'm simply being absurd. So that your own natural sense of outraged logic can bring you to your senses."

"Well, I'm not buying any of this crap," Norman said angrily.

"Oh, come on," Harry exclaimed. "Don't you have any sense of fun left in you, somewhere in there, way down deep? Haven't you read any fairytales, any fiction of wonder and the imagination, when you were alive? Remember what weird stuff happens to people in those stories?"

"So, God uses the phrase 'weird stuff' and literary references. If you were God you wouldn't need to ask me things, you'd know," Norman persisted. "You wouldn't talk down to me like that. You wouldn't have—*expectations* of me. And you'd be—different."

"I'm merely teasing you, Norman. *Never testing —always teasing*. I do know. I *can* be different. Take a joke, will ya? For old times' sake." Harry smiled at him.

"What old times? Time is what I no longer have, old or new! I'm dead! Before that, I've been a very sick dying old man for about six years! I've forgotten what it means to take a joke or to make one. So what the hell do you want from me? What kind of a God are you?"

"I see," God-woman said. "You are feeling sorry for yourself. That's perfectly fine, your—ahem— God-given right. Unfortunately, Norman, you'll have to do that a bit later, on your own time, when you make your stay either in Heaven or Hell. But now—you and I are here together for a different reason."

"What?"

The woman-God-Harry looked around, rubbed her hands together, and took a big breath. "Here's your big chance, Norman. Ask me any question. Any question about anything that you've ever wanted answered. Because here's my big chance to answer it for you."

"Fine," Norman Jones said, smirking. "What is the Meaning of Life?"

"Quite simple, actually. The meaning of life is to reconstruct Humpty Dumpty. But first, you must find out all the Rules of the Universe, the Order and the inherent Pattern. You must discover Truth, and accrue Experience. Of course, the more you learn, the more Rules are revealed, the wider the vista of knowledge, and the more difficult it becomes to organize the knowledge into a coherent pattern. But that is the final Challenge—for later."

"And that—" Norman smirked again, "—is why you are such a divine jerk. That's just a bunch of big incoherent words. Besides, surely it's been said before, by someone, some philosophical demagogue in stuffy halls of academia. . . ."

"*Incoherent*, did you say?" God interrupted.

"Why, Norman, then you must have some idea when there is coherency present, right? You do recognize 'meaning' when you encounter it?"

"Trick question. Should I say yes or no? Will either make me a lesser idiot? Fine then, I'll brave it. Yes. Of course I am aware of 'meaning.' Otherwise, we wouldn't be discussing it."

"In that case, deep inside, by instinct, and because you're not an idiot, you already know the answer. Next question!"

"But—"

"Next question, Norman!"

"All right! That wasn't fair, but—why is there so much suffering in the world? Why do wonderful, gentle, good people starve, die, live lives of poverty and misery, while murderers, rapists, sociopaths, and overall assholes thrive? Why are there wars? Why disease—AIDS, cancer? Why are there broken families, unwanted children, old parents, the homeless? Why do some people believe in Jesus, others in Yahweh, others in Allah, others in Nothing, others in Science, others in the Dollar, and others simply kill in the name of whatever deity they choose? Why is history one long blood bath? Why are we all afraid of the unknown, and therefore hate those who are different from us? Why does money buy so much, while love seems to get you only rejection and broken hearts? Why did my daughter Anne get divorced three times? Why did my little boy Jimmy who once had angelic eyes, abuse his wife and children, ending up in a mental hospital? Why am I—"

Norman's tirade dwindled. *Never bring up the self....*

"Why, why, why. Why must we speak in so many clichés? Do you realize," God responded, "that you merely question specific effects upon specific individuals or groups, *within limited context?* So easy to do that, right, Norman? So easy to wax poetic and righteous! Such a popular pastime for conventional intellectuals in your former life's culture of *angst* and egocentric, sadomasochistic, orgasm-based, meaningless individuality! And yet, my friend, it all comes down to finding a single, cut, long-stemmed rose lying on a tabletop and wondering—like a lackwit—where it came from! Why is it cut, why the thorns, why is it red? A phenomenon torn out of Universal context."

"So . . . I am now a lackwit. And my question—or pardon me, my phrasing of the question—sucks. Maybe. But only because you made me that way. My thanks to you, God. But—no need to patronize, I understand it. Back where I came from they used to call it cause and effect . . ." Norman muttered quietly.

"I know you know, my beloved lackwit-who-is-not," God said. "And it is precisely why you must now take cause and effect a step further. Tie each cause and effect relationship together with ALL the others, and then, *find a common thread that runs through all*. Invoke your talent for analogy."

"So, what are you getting at?"

The woman-Harry-God went silent for a moment. She looked in his eyes, her own expression mundane and human, and simply waited.

Norman wanted to fidget at the silence. "Are you expecting me to say something?" he muttered finally, in an irritated voice that had in it also a primal hurt, the same vulnerability that he'd shown to his mother alone, only once, somewhere, long ago. . . . When he still believed in warmth.

And then God smiled.

"I was simply giving you some time to think. But since your thoughts refuse to focus, and wander to other things, I'll give you a hint in answer to your question about suffering: if you were to tie together all the cause and effect relationships that you mentioned, *and* all the ones that you didn't—and aren't even aware of—then, you will see that—brace yourself here, Norman—

you'll see that *directly I have nothing to do with any of it*.

"The only thing I am responsible for, Norman, is the original Pattern. The Way. The Rules. The direction of Energy. That includes the pattern and way and rules of Change, or Movement. Because, believe it or not, that's all the Universe is—variously moving energy!"

"Big deal . . ." Norman said. "I thought that's what Physics has been telling us all along."

"Quite right," God said. "Physics, or Science, are just labels that describe an organized human response to the Universe. This very same response is described by others as Religion. Both perspectives are valid—but only as specific limited terms, not universal answers. In fact, I don't like either, because they tend to *exclude* rather than *include* concepts. And because there are so many emotionally charged connotations attached to them that actually prevent everyone from pursuing the real truth."

"And what would that be? Truth. What's truth?"

"That'll be your next question," God said. "Let me finish the first. We were speaking of Rules, or Limits. I am the Creator, and therefore Rulemaker. I provide the game board, the game pieces, and the allowed moves—such as chess. The rest is up to you. However, unlike chess, I don't create pawns and kings, humble or exalted, yet fixed in their original state and function. My game pieces start out all the same—primal energy moving of its own Free Will, and yet within the almost unnoticeable confinement of my Rules, or what you sometimes refer to as 'Fate'—a silly loaded word, by the way.

"Thus, primal energy may evolve or devolve, mutate from a quickly moving state (energy) to a slowly moving state (matter)—all of this never being a question of 'good' or 'bad,' 'ahead' or 'behind,' but simply 'closer' or 'farther' from the end Goal of learning the Rules or discovering Limits, then using the absolute knowledge acquired to find the Next Step."

"So you're saying you're not responsible for innocent children developing Multiple Sclerosis?" exclaimed Norman.

"There you go again, being specific and out of context. Sometimes," God said, "I get frustrated with the limitations of my own set Rules, such as that of language, in our case. For, I would like to give you multiple answers all at once, to your question. But, Rules of linear communication prevent me. And of course, there is a reason for these Rules, because you are at the point in your evolution where you still require such linear flow of logic. And I must comply, by responding to only one logical thread at a time. So, I'll pick up this one. . . .

"What is meant by 'innocent?' Another loaded word. Innocence, just as guilt, is relative. And it does not mean what you think it means. It is easy to see only a child from the moment of its birth without considering the adult that the child *was* or *will be*. Just as it is easy to condemn a murderer or rapist for their self-hate that has been turned outward into violence, without knowing the origins of that violence. There is only one thing I can say to that, Norman, and both you and I know it's been said before—no one is qualified to judge until one is completely aware of the full extent of the situation. Since I, being the Rulemaker, am the only one aware of the full set of Rules and Limits and Parameters, the only one who knows the whole picture, then I am the only Judge. And it is left up to each individual to discover, after you discover All, the true nature of the 'Judgment' I render.

"However, I do not limit you from judging within your own scope. In fact, without the ability to judge or appraise the immediate environment, you would not be able to make the next move. But you may judge only as long as you know your scope and limits. And as long as you allow that there is more to everything than what you perceive.

"And my answer to all of your spoken and unspoken questions so far is both 'yes' and 'no.' I am responsible in the absolute sense, but not relative. I am responsible for forming you from my own energy-self, but I have no part in the actual direction your self first took eons ago, once it found Individuality."

"I don't buy your idea of responsibility . . ." muttered Norman, "Answer me straight, *why is there suffering?*"

"For one thing, because there *is* Individuality. It implies an active will, a moving vector, a living arrow shot into the great Dark. When differently moving vectors collide, there is a conflict of will. And the more resistance, the more effort is required to continue moving in the direction of choice. Effort is a natural response generated in reaction to resistance and obstacles in one's way—a defense mechanism used by the will to maintain itself, its precious sense of individuality, its very *direction*.

"At this stage of the Universal Cycle of movement, the Pendulum is on an outward swing—the Universe is chaotic and expanding, and Order, or Union, requires greater effort. It's tough enough to maintain individuality while pursuing an aimless course of your own choosing, regardless of the rest of the Universe—indeed, at its most basic, it is simple self-preservation and *survival*. And self-preservation, in its most amoral, raw state, is occasionally referred to as 'Evil.'

"Now, imagine how much more difficult it is, Norman, to maintain not just your individual course but at the same time to take into account the movement of everyone else! It's a matter of deftly navigating between obstacles, or just plowing through them! The struggle to navigate the chaos of the immediate surroundings, of other teeming souls, is the perfect energy generator of life, a closed circuit of cause and effect—the only true universal paradox. Effort builds momentum, focuses the will, and results in a displacement of energy which is the stuff of life, and which is accompanied by pain.

"And this brings us to the definition of 'Good' and 'Evil,' even if you haven't asked. After all, these concepts are fundamentally intertwined. 'Good' acts along a course of least harm, regardless of personal suffering, taking into consideration all the rest of the Universe. 'Evil' attempts to avoid pain and as a result causes it in others around it, so that eventually it also suffers by association.

"Often, both 'Good' and 'Evil' is associated with strong will and clear direction. However that notion is misleading. 'Good' strives for order and cohesion, for eventual *union*, despite the expanding Universe, while 'Evil' strives for one's own personal desire to survive the immediate moment, without considering the long term, and aimlessly rides the wave of individualistic momentum. That's why sometimes those who are evil may do incidental good—if it happens to incidentally benefit their selfish course—and the good may cause temporary evil—if they are severely limited by the circumstances."

"Please, enough! Enough about suffering! This may be off the subject," Norman blurted out, "but can you please clarify once and for all whether sex is good or evil?"

In answer, God laughed.

Actually God went on laughing for quite some time, a nice ringing and yet booming androgynous laughter that eventually became soft chuckles, and then echo. . . .

"Seriously, you need to ask?" God finally said. "Norman—sex is just a tool. If you ask whether any tool is good or bad—the answer is the same. It depends on how well it's made. And it depends on its function."

"Okay . . ." gulped Norman, who really just needed a small break.

"We're getting to the end of our discussion here, bear with me," God said. "And by the way, I hope you realize that I always see through bullshit."

And for the last time, God-woman-Harry became serious.

"You had originally asked me if I am Satan. That, Norman, is the *only* question I may not answer you. For, it would involve giving away one of the most important concepts that you need to grasp on your own. Finding out what is 'Satan' is part of your task of putting together Humpty Dumpty after the Fall. Thus, I may not 'cheat' and give away the answer, except to say that there are indeed two modes— 'Good' and 'Evil, 'effort' and 'indifference'—and to warn you that they are not easily distinguishable when taken out of Universal context.

"But—let me conclude this simply, and in the process make you smile—Humpty Dumpty is the Universe. Finding pieces of Humpty Dumpty, putting them together again, and discovering that you are one of those pieces, is the meaning of life. Suffering is when you yourself don't realize that you're a piece of Humpty Dumpty, don't realize *which* piece you are, can't seem to find the right other pieces that fit the jigsaw right next to you, can't seem to put the pieces together, or when other pieces suddenly acquire a will of their own and don't want to be joined. What a mess, no wonder there's suffering! But notice: in the end, after you've tried a million times, given up, fallen apart, raged and wept and died and fallen, and struggled all over again, the Universal goal—unlike Humpty Dumpty—is pieced together. Simply because the final Rule is that of Union, Completion, Oneness. In the human mindset it is occasionally referred to as—and unfortunately limited by—the term 'Love.'"

Norman listened to this, and was suddenly aware that his very thoughts were *burning*. He stared at the ordinary looking woman before him who was *not*, and his vision kept on going in and out of focus. One instant he would see a great haze-lit hall, and the next, he glimpsed a Cosmic panorama of black velvet nothingness and eternal stars.

"Crap!" said Norman, and took hold of his head. "Seriously, I can't take any more of this concept stuff—God or whatever you are. . . ."

"Don't you want to ask me what Truth is?"

"At this point I couldn't care less. Tell me later. . . . I need to use the spiritual bathroom . . . and maybe a spiritual vomit bag. . . ."

"No you don't, Norman. But it's obvious that you've reached your absolute limit of *ingestion* and are ready to *process* and *digest*. So I'll let you go now. Until later—"

And as unexpectedly as possible, God and everything around Norman was gone.

· · ·

THE FERRIS WHEEL TURNED SLOWLY, lights blinking. Norman stood on a street corner of someplace that looked absolutely like an amusement park, and watched the two-seat cars carry passengers higher and higher, and then back down again, in a kind of mellow after-dinner stupor. Thirtyish, and in long pajamas, he was licking a giant Raspberry-Truffle-Vanilla-Bean ice-cream cone. He was absolutely fulfilled, and only now allowed his thoughts to blossom, emerging as though out of a dream.

There were people everywhere, people of all ages. Some hurried to and fro, others loitered easily, and yet others were like sleep-walkers, chewing mauve cotton candy with blank eyes, or emerging from a colorful neon souvenir store-front with armfuls of teddy bears or charming old-fashioned knick-knacks. Their eyes held translucent dreams, all. What did they see, these people, thought Norman, what did they really see?

The same things I am seeing now?

There was a lot of soft, sincere laughter coming from all sides—not the contrived harsh laughter that he had once been accustomed to hearing, or the false social cackle that calls attention to its trendy self—this laughter was somehow gentle, subdued, and intimately private. It seemed to be coming from the inside, like happy champagne bubbles, and often the one who laughed was alone, sharing a private joke with only oneself.

Norman thought that this was awfully like his idea of a gentle sanitarium for the mentally ill. But his instinct hinted that it was simply a place where "adults" suddenly no longer possessed the attribute of age, and so could be children or ancients simultaneously.

"Hi there, you're fully awake now, aren't you?" came a voice from his left, and Norman turned to see a tall thirteen-year-old girl with freckles and soft orange-gold hair.

"What's your name?" she said. "Or, rather, what would you like to be called?"

"Norman J. Jones." And then he added, still dazed. "But I've always wanted to be called 'Antonio.'"

"Then Antonio you are!" said the girl. "You may call me Margaret. I used to be called Marge all these seventy years or so before I—died, and I always hated it—so unglamorous. Margaret is so much more dignified, don't you think? I like Margaret. I also like being a teenager—I've never stopped feeling like one anyway, even at seventy. You feel thirty, I see."

"I what?" Norman-Antonio said, as he unconsciously felt the vigor of his young muscled body. "So, we're all dead, and we can conveniently be any age we like. Are we in Hell or is this the commercialized neon version of Heaven?"

"Hold it!" Margaret laughed. "I can't believe you're still in a philosophical mood. Cynical, too. Wow. God must've worked you over and done a number on you. Scared you real good, eh? 'Scared good'—I suppose that's bad grammar, right? Wrong? Hah, who cares! And did God also give you that Humpty Dumpty spiel in the very end? I rather liked it—did you?" And she giggled some more. "My dear darling dearie, Antonio-Tonio, I'm feeling silly and thirteen, I have no cares, and I just wanna scream, NOW!"

And she did scream. She let out a piercing happy shriek, and then spun around in a giddy circle on one foot, and then skipped and galloped back and forth in front of him, rather like a four-year-old than a thirteen year-old. No one paid them the least bit of attention.

"You still haven't answered my question," Antonio-Norman persisted in a soft voice, brushing back dark hair with a gesture he hadn't used in forty years, mostly for lack of said hair. "Is this Heaven or Hell?"

Margaret stopped skipping. Breathing fast she came up to his face, stuck her tongue out, and turned her head from side to side, all the meanwhile staring at him.

"What do you think?" she said.

"I don't know. . . . It appears to be a place of freedom, which implies Heaven. And yet, *no apparent restrictions* implies chaos, or Hell. So does the great amount of sensually appealing—uh—things."

"Like ice cream?" Margaret grinned. "And have you screwed anyone yet?" She crinkled her face into an even greater smirk. "You *can*, you know. I did, before I decided to forego my roaring twenties and permanently regress to thirteen. Oh, did I shock you? My, I'm a dirty old woman, am I not?" And again she giggled.

Antonio was beginning to think he didn't really like this Margaret. Or, did he? Confusing.

"We were speaking—"

"Awww, all right, I'll tell you," said the old-young woman-girl. "It's neither Heaven nor Hell. That comes *later*. For now, this whole—place—if you'd like to call it that—is LIFE, Incorporated. The free place *in-between*. I think?"

"I thought that was Purgatory. . . . Sorry, a Judeo-Christian concept, I'm still stuck in the old mindset. I suppose there's still so much I have to learn here . . ."

he muttered. "And you too. If I may ask, Margaret, when did you—die?"

"That question used to bother me at first, but now I don't care that much. If you mean in what earth century, you must tell me what century you died in, first. One of the unwritten Rules here—yes, there are Rules—is that unless we are from the same approximate time, we may not correctly communicate about our past lives to those who lived chronologically before us."

"Twentieth century, the nineties," he said.

"Hah, I beat you! Twenty-third century. Sorry I cannot tell you anything, then."

"So!" Antonio exclaimed. "Then my hunch is right, and all these people really are from different times, which proves to me that time does not exist indeed, and that all of it is relative and absolute bullshit! By the way, I seriously would love for you to tell me something about the 23rd Century, please! Is the environment depleted? Any EMP disasters? Global warming? Asteroid extinction events? Is humanity still around? I'd be frankly surprised."

"Do I look to you like a *homo sapiens*, or a duckbill platypus? Doesn't my being here answer your question about humanity still being around? But really, Tony. I can't tell you any more, silly man-boy. You won't hear or understand me. Believe me, I've tried it with others. There was this really neat guy from the Middle Ages, twelfth century A.D., and we couldn't speak a word of anything but gibberish, the minute I began to tell him things. Funny thing, I could understand his personal stories of the past with no problem."

"That doesn't sound—believable."

"It doesn't? Well, here, let me tell you about the 23rd Century life in !@#$%^&*() !@#$%^&*() !@#$%^&*()," Margaret said. "!@#$%^&*()."

She was speaking in tongues.

"Sweet Jesus," said Antonio-who-was-Norman, "I'm not sure I can deal with this after all. . . . And to think that back *there* people are afraid of just being dead with nothing to look forward to but dark non-existence in the end. If this is how afterlife is, then I'd rather take Vacuum!"

"No you wouldn't. In a Vacuum, you wouldn't *exist*. Really, I think you meant to say you might like to take a Valium instead. Poor baby boy. You're just getting to face a veritable flood of nasty controversial quasi-theoretical quantum realities, that's all. We all go through it. I mean, I did, at first. . . ."

As Norman-Antonio watched her, he noticed that throughout the last five minutes Margaret was gently and almost imperceptibly beginning to age. Shimmering, her form lost the gawkiness of childhood, rounded out, and he found himself staring at a pair of breasts tightly outlined against her blouse.

Noticing the direction of his look, Margaret suddenly blushed like fine wine. "Oops," she said. "It's actually hard for me to maintain thirteen. I think that all of us are basically in our prime, thirtyish, like you are."

"So, there is no time . . ." Norman said. He really did feel like himself again. Antonio was just a glamorous heroic personality that he used to fantasize about and imagine being as a kid, but which suddenly felt funny to him, heroic rippling muscles and all.

And now the glamour was gone.

"You really look like a Norman now," Margaret said, looking him up and down. "Yes, very much a *Norman.*"

"I know." he said. "That's who I am."

They stood around for a while, watching others, watching the Ferris Wheel, the lights, the colors, the soft atmosphere of pleasure. There wasn't really a sky, but Norman had a sudden feeling of evening descending, a quelling of sorts.

Margaret must have felt it too. "Have you checked in yet?" she said suddenly.

"What do you mean? Where?"

"Into Heaven or Hell, that's where. Like into a hotel. You must, before the end of your first day."

"There are days here. . . ?" he echoed.

"Of course. There's no setting sun, but you just get a feeling of completion at the end of each of your personal days, and then you go to bed."

"For some reason," Norman continued, "I just didn't really believe in Heaven or in Hell. I still don't. I can't see how either can make sense. . . ."

"And, they don't. But, regardless of whether you believe or not, they *are*. But they're—*different*. Not what you think. You'll see. Come on!"

And now that she mentioned it, Norman could see, somewhere beyond the looming Ferris Wheel, another large neon sign, which he recognized to be the backside of the LIFE, INC. sign. (*So, I am inside the endlessly-mutating building*, he thought.) The sign said: HEAVEN AND HELL (TM). And it winked on and off every couple of seconds, coming up in red and then in green lights.

It was calling him home.

THE FRONT LOBBY was softly-lit and elegantly comfortable. Norman felt himself dozing off on his feet, as he stood behind Margaret at the Reception Desk. Margaret was talking to a pleasant older gentleman at the desk, wearing a pin-striped suit and sporting a mustache. "Keys to room H-23781, please." she was saying. "And also, this person is new, so he needs to check in."

The old gentleman pulled out a curious archaic gold-rimmed monocle on a fine chain and, placing it over his left eye, squinted at Norman. For several long moments he seemed to be closely perusing something, studying Norman silently. "Hmmm . . . All right . . ." he muttered in a slightly trembling old person voice.

Next, the gentleman replaced the monocle over his right eye, and proceeded to study Norman again, through the lens. Finally, just as Norman was getting slightly edgy, the gentleman said: "Fine, fine . . ."

And then, as though remembering a very vital thing, he suddenly coughed in embarrassment, and exclaimed "Oh dear, I'm so sorry, I forgot to introduce myself, oh dear. . . ."

Norman introduced himself first. "I am Norman J. Jones. Or at least, that's what I was back there."

Reaching out a wrinkled hand, the old one shook Norman's slightly limp hand. "Allow me to welcome you, dear Mr. Jones—Norman—here, to Life Incorporated's *Heaven and Hell*, a fine establishment. To you, my friend, I am the Honorable Peter, once a Fisherman, and most familiar to those such as yourself as one of the Twelve who followed the One referred to as the Christ. To others unfamiliar with Christ, I am also *another*, but that is somewhat irrelevant. Now, Norman, I have looked at you with my Right Eye, to measure you for Heaven, and with my Left, to measure you for Hell. Having made my conclusions, I assign you to room H-23095, 7th floor, to your right."

"So," said Norman, "What does that mean?"

"It means that you get a room, stupid," Margaret said.

"I *mean*," Norman said in a cool voice, "where is room H-23095? In Heaven or Hell?"

"Neither, dear Norman. Or rather, not quite. The rooms are not exactly *located* as you might normally assume. You see, each room is in the same neutral state when it is first occupied. But it will change. And it is *you* who will determine the direction and progress of its nature."

"Okay . . ." said Norman, "So—"

"So take your keys and let's go, please!" Margaret was bouncing up and down in agitation.

"But," Norman said sullenly, "I still don't understand, am I in Heaven or Hell, dammit?! Where did you assign me?"

"Whatever you do, my friend, don't swear,

please," said the Honorable Peter. "And I'm not just saying it like a stuffy Sunday school teacher who just *forbade* and never explained why. As a matter of fact, when you utter anything Norman, especially *here*, your words represent a focused will, and therefore, power. They mold reality—any reality within your reach. So be careful, or you may really 'damn' someone or something—whatever 'damn' may truly mean to your personal way of thinking."

"That's right," Margaret said. "Listen to him." Now that Norman thought about it, she was quite whimsical in the way she took upon herself the authority of this place. But she was still awfully annoying.

"And to answer your question—I simply assigned you to a room," said the old gentleman who called himself the Honorable Peter, smiling lightly, and offered a pair of plain brass keys to Norman. He then nodded to signify that for the time being he had nothing more to say.

Margaret was pulling Norman by the hand, toward the elevator.

The elevator was already packed. However, Norman and the on-again, off-again teenager found themselves flattened tightly against the side wall, as more and more people, appearing as though out of nowhere, got in right behind them, wearing and carrying all kinds of crazy and unimaginable things. And with a pleasant ding, the elevator proceeded to stop on every floor, loading and unloading human livestock.

They finally collapsed outside the elevator door on Floor Seven.

"So, are we now in seventh heaven?" Norman said with a sarcastic smile. "Or is it the seventh circle of hell?"

"Your room must be that way, over there." Margaret pointed down the hall. "Mine's right nearby on the same floor. This place is huge...."

And then she turned to look at him, glancing fully in the eyes, saying: "Go to bed, tired old man. Get some rest before the rest of eternity."

The look of her eyes was unreadable, and yet, in its vagueness, hinted at intense, scalding truth.

NORMAN OPENED the door to his room, and in the blackness, felt around for a light switch.

So, it's neither heaven nor hell. I am in limbo, he thought with dry cynicism. And then, *Well. How morally predictable. My own being, my actions, not only determine but literally shape my eternal sentence. I should have thought of that myself.*

And in that instant, as though invoked by a spirit

of the air, sourceless, the lights came on, and Norman gasped.

He was in Paradise.

Actually it all resembled his idea of an exotic palace-harem, somewhere in the Middle or Far East of his life's memories, with Hinduistic overtones and touches of the mystical in its overwhelming vibrant color and splendor.

Not merely a room, but a lush frescoed hall of marble, gold, and precious stone inlay. Lofty dome ceiling floating high above, somewhere, dreamy, in clouds of incense, lavender, acacias, and sensual musk—or was it the scent of sacred Myrrh? Columns of wrought encrusted gems. . . . Lapis-lazuli and mountain crystal winking in crevices of plied soft gold. . . . Statues of beautiful voluptuous beings of androgynous sensuality and paradox-purity. . . . The lulling sound of trickling water. . . . A warm breeze from some distant, nonexistent place *outside*. . . .

Before him, reclined a great high bed, strewn with deep violet satin and forest-green silk, with pillows like a baby's cheek, smooth, pale, shimmering. Above it, a canopy, and pale gauze and lace, wafting on the breeze. . . .

This was his room!

And in the consequent instant Norman had ceased questioning, ceased attempting to see logical connections, or meaningful sides to things, ceased to care whether heaven or hell or anything that bore a human name surrounded him now.

He was in the deepest Pit or highest Pinnacle, but all he knew was that he was home at last. Or so his senses screamed.

And Norman J. Jones plunged in.

He was hardly aware of himself, whether he swooned naked upon the silk, whether the silk came to drift gently from above, from all sides, and hide him, like a cocoon of abandon, or whether his perception distorted and pulsed like a heartbeat, while he simply lay down or fell down upon air itself that formed and re-formed into vibrant matter all around him like a living mist.

He was also never sure if he dreamed that a woman came to him, with pliant limbs of flesh-satin and the receptive eyes of a doe . . . eyes that somehow resembled his ancient once-so-long-ago love. The *houri* lay down next to him, beside him, on the satin and silk and pillows, just out of reach, so that he could just feel the warmth of her warmth, and the heat of her golden aura—but he could not touch.

For centuries it seemed they remained thus, locked in a nearness that seemed more aphrodisiac than his human imagination could ever conceive. For, as they lay, he *created* her in his mind, every detail, every point and smooth warm softness of her, going over and over, until he burned, lying immobilized and molten and hard, his solar plexus like a blossom of fire, and on the verge of something that was like the sun, incandescent and burning white....

WHEN HE AWOKE—OR came to himself—it was his personal morning.

Norman found himself lying in a pleasant bed-and-breakfast hotel room, full of small unique touches that brought to mind nostalgic moments of his past, of all the beds and bedrooms he'd ever been in, of all he had seen on television, read about in books, or fantasized in the twilight hours bordering between wakefulness and sleep. Getting up, he discovered that if he focused, he could see a door to the bathroom that literally formed out of the blank wall. He could also focus on himself, his pajamas, he noticed, and make things *change*. He stared, concentrating on the visual lines and flow of fabric, and the instant he did, he was wearing other clothes, all kinds of clothes. Outfits appeared to change on him with a mercurial yet hazy outpouring of form, the moment his memories touched upon such. Soon, Norman literally focused into existence a mirror—

very solid, very functional, very specific—creating it before him out of the very mist. He then preened himself before it like a peacock, in imperial outfits from the Chinese Ming Dynasty, in golden foppish attire of Louis IV the Sun King, in orthodox priestly robes of velvet and gold, in ancient Greek armor of burnished metal, then Medieval knight armor, and ended by wearing the khaki green of Desert Storm and holding an AK-47. He did notice however that all the costumes he modeled were somehow imperfect, unreal—only as detailed as his memories would allow.

His next thought was of food. He had not been hungry up to that point, but it suddenly occurred to him that he *should* be.

A turn of his eye, a half-glance, and a feast was before him, laid out on a table that wasn't there only a second ago. All his favorite things were piled upon platters and serving dishes and deep bowls—foods that brought in-rushing waves of memories, of childhood and softness and basic comfort that Norman forgot all about. Or maybe, he had lost track of it so long ago, even longer than he thought. And with the lost memories, had gone the faint flicker of trust that was once a solid flame in his embryonic newborn consciousness.

Norman remembered that trust-flame suddenly,

the flickering warmth that could be like a miniature personal sun if allowed to burn unchecked. Once, somewhere, eons ago, it had warmed his center with a contentment that made him confident always, unwavering in his recognition of truth all around him. It was this missing trust that now made him unsure, made him cynical, and made him question all motives, most of all his own.

Norman remembered all this, and at the same time gorged himself on the ethereal food, never knowing what passed his lips, only the way it felt at the back of his throat at the moment of swallowing—solid, definite, fulfilling. The ever-present bottomless abyss inside was being filled with the substance of unquenched dreams.

Just as suddenly, it was all gone. He was not sure if it was satiation or boredom, but the actual *reality* of the things around Norman began to flicker, fade, probably because he came to the conclusion that he had no significant need to maintain it. No need to exert effort.

Norman found himself in a white padded cell.

It was simply that he had ceased to *remember*, and the thought images of his past no longer had enough impact to materialize and transform the environment around him.

He sat down on the floor of the cell, legs

sprawled out, upon the soft haze-white padding. Then, he lay completely. Ah, what soft pillows!

And it seemed to him for a moment only, that he was lying on softly sparkling snow. It was the powder of faerie, shimmering lavender, azure, and indigo under the warm peach golden shadow-light of faintly glowing street lanterns—somewhere in a childhood of his long-ago. And overhead, the moon was full, skating like a New Year ice-queen on the frozen pond of heaven-velvet.

There was no time, no movement, only peace. Norman lost the thin thread of consciousness, and then again regained it. . . . And again. . . . Over and over, endlessly. . . . Over and over he ceased to exist, lulled by the Universal absolute peace. When he occasionally came to, out of that deathly absoluteness, it was only due to a whisper of some memory that would suddenly surface and pull him with it.

At those times he found himself re-living the memory, joining its momentum. He would wake in a sparse forest glade, in fragrant clumps of grass, while the wind of high summer moved millions of tiny green leaves high above, sweeping in chartreuse and gold sparkles across the face of the zenith sun. And with each surge of the breeze, the grass hummed with insect song, while from the green-clad hills in the distance, sounded haunting echoes of wild birds, speeding high overhead. . . .

He would blank out and then find himself floating on the ocean, glittering blue-green and mirror-bright like a thousand broken razor-shards of light. The deep shadowed water covered him with cool completeness, holding him buoyant and smooth, while the spray filled the air with the very scent of life. He tread the water effortlessly, never seeing the shore, nor the incandescent sun beating from overhead—for his vision back then had been weak, and he saw only shapes of color without his corrective lenses. But it did not matter that he did not see, only that he was filled with an exuberance, with a sudden passion to move, to act, a welling of the life-force, of unbridled pure *desire* of the spirit. . . .

Norman came to himself with a start, jerked into being by that sense of desire, which he now realized to be the true antithesis of death. He found himself lying in the same vaguely familiar composite-memory hotel room. And he got up from the bed, focused on a doorway, finding his assigned pair of brass keys hanging next to the suddenly apparent light-switch. Turning the door handle, he flicked off the light-switch, and left room H-23095, to venture into LIFE, INC.

. . .

NORMAN PAUSED to wipe the sweat off his brow as he momentarily set down the hammer and chisel, and stared at the shape forming before him out of the dull reddish metal.

The statue was of a human male shape, the head still unformed, three quarters real size. Norman had always wanted to try sculpting in his spare time. But since he always found his desire to do so grow suddenly weak when any opportunity came up, he had never gotten a chance to do it. But now, the workshop around him—a place wrought with the force of his mind, a place that had hazy perimeters, no walls, and an unreal light-source—held several dozen statues and relief groups made by his own hand. The first ones of these, the early ones, made in the first personal weeks of his presence *here*, were attempts to copy the Masters.

The first two were pathetic tries. He continued working on them however, being aware of their sad, graceless state, their primitive angularity, all throughout, and yet also aware of what he *could* do, *would* do, very soon, driven with the relentlessness of creative desire.

That *knowledge* of what he would do eventually, of what he was capable of, was the only thing forcing him forward. While the creative desire, he realized, was but the need for perfection, for the ideal, for utter beauty realized. So, it was not merely *desire* that moved him, but the confidence in his ability to fulfill that desire—a confidence that was not there before he started, but had been created, a gratifying surprise, through the very process of strife, like the Botticelli Venus from the sea foam.

The third of his attempts succeeded. Athena, Goddess of War and Wisdom stood before him, wrought in steel, three fifths to scale of the original marble Athena Giustiniani seen in the Vatican, dressed in a layered tunic and helmet, holding a brass spear, and at her feet, a coiled serpent. A thrill of *something* almost sexual went through him to see the cool beauty of her forming, the fact that there was the same grace in her lines, the same living curves, as in the original of marble. Since then, he had copied five more ancient masterpieces, and on the sixth one, surpassed the original, and ceased copying.

And as Norman continued to work, through weeks and months of personal days, he was also aware that his hands striking and forcing the tools no longer felt pain, the bruises from the hammer missing the target and instead hitting his knuckles, were faded, his swollen-blue fingers misshapen no longer.

He had also ceased feeling sweat on his brow, and soon, ceased knowing that he had a forehead to wipe. He worked absolutely entranced, from pure memory, and created out of marble, brass, wax, steel, iron, wood, and precious stones, beauty that he had not even seen, only dreamed of in his life.

And one personal day, it was all over. Norman put the finishing touches on an exquisite miniature three-inch replica of a German Gothic cathedral made of jasper, with moving doors, and real filigree stained glass windows of crystal. Then he glanced at the beauty of form before him. And the desire left him.

But no, it was not the desire for perfection, for beauty. It was simply the desire to create beauty *in this specific manner*.

Norman's attention wandered, his will unfocused, diffused, and he suddenly found himself wandering a now-familiar yet ever-mutating street of LIFE, INC., with the sight of the Ferris Wheel in the distance. Norman realized that he would always come here when it was his personal time to rest from one manner of activity. This was the brief respite, before a desire of another sort would take hold of him and whip him into a passion, a flurry of action.

At that point, Margaret came up to him from behind, and poked his lower back with one long tapering thirtyish finger. Norman jumped at the auric touch—for he knew now that all was spirit here—and then he felt the warmth of familiarity, of contact.

"Do you believe in twin souls?" Margaret asked him point-blank, with no other introduction.

He'd been ready to commence with the usual "Hello-How-are-you-What-have-you-done-since." According to his personal reckoning, it's been long since he had seen her. Instead, he said sheepishly, "What? Oh, well—do you think that maybe you and I—are?"

"Of course not," she said—and he remembered how irritating she could be. "All I said, Norman-Dude, was a question. Do you believe in twin souls? I'm just asking."

"Well," he began, "I suppose, I used to once, when I was twenty and alive. There was even a woman I had known very briefly, that would have almost been what you call, a soul twin. For a while we had been intimate to the level where I believed I understood her and she understood me, all the way. But it wasn't so, not all the way. Not to the quick. . . . We drifted apart, ended up friends and then distant, because when it came down to it, there was no such thing as unconditional acceptance, no matter how close we came. And now—I'm just not sure."

"Well, I don't believe in twin souls," Margaret stated, very businesslike. "I believe instead in soul triplets."

Norman laughed. "Explain," he said.

The thirtyish woman jumped up and down like a thirteen-year-old. "Oh, Norman, do you really care to know? You mean it? Well, this is my theory: If, like God tried to beat it into our heads, we're all pieces of one whole, pieces of a great jigsaw, and if we're all at different stages of development, then it would only make sense that each one of us, each individual entity, fits into the great whole so that some other entity comes just before and just after. Just think of a line of people holding hands—Someone is holding your right, and someone is holding your left, one being just a little ahead, supporting and leading you, and one being just a little behind, whom you support and lead—and so on. So there is still the concept of soul twins, except that there are two twins for each being, and depending on which one you meet, you will either spiritually lead or follow."

"Maybe that is the Christian mystery of the Trinity," Norman said. "Maybe...."

"Whatever," Margaret said. "Now, enough serious stuff. We may not be twin souls, but we must be pretty close in the lineup, because we seem to understand each other pretty well, don't you agree?"

"I suppose," he said.

"So now," said she, "now that *that's* out of the way—'cause I like to do all things backwards—Hi, Norman! What have you been up to, what have you done? How's LIFE, INC. treated you?"

"If you shut up for a moment, I'll tell you." He grinned. "But first, how about a ride on the Ferris Wheel? Come on!"

MARGARET TOLD him that since she'd first *died* and come here, she had been a Classical ballerina, a juggler, had made Medieval Gobelin-style tapestries, became a first-rate fencer—both with the French foil and saber—and then learned how to work Damask steel into fine-bladed weapons of the Crusades. Next, she learned architecture, and designed futuristic structures of plexi-glass. Then, in one of the narrow cozy streets of LIFE, INC., she had wandered upon a miracle of miracles—the ancient great Library of Alexandria, once destroyed in a fire, and with it all the early human knowledge of Truth. Here, she spent what probably was an eternity, reading. . . . Finally, her last months—"Yes, months!" she exclaimed—were taken up with fiber-optics and electrical engineering.

"So how long did all this take, exactly?" Norman said. "Does it mean I have to do all these things too?"

"Actually, I have no idea," she responded flippantly, as she dangled her feet off the Ferris Wheel seat, at least a hundred feet in the air.

"And," he persisted carefully, "how much longer will it be?"

"Eternity, probably. There's no time." Margaret yawned pleasantly. "Why are you asking me? I have no clue. We're in the same rowboat, remember?"

"What really concerns me," Norman persisted, half to himself, "is whether it is our desires that force us to pursue these things. I mean, why else would I be sculpting non-stop, and now that I think about, hardly pausing to rest or sleep? And then suddenly, I lose all interest, and here I am."

"Well, you probably achieved what you set out to do, quicker than you would have ever done on earth, unhindered by the very act of living. That's why the urge was gone."

"And what might that urge lead me to do next? And then what? Will there ever be an end to it? Is that what afterlife is all about? Creativity? Developing your potential?"

"Why not?"

"I'll tell you why not! Because that's too good to be true! Heaven . . . One-sided . . . What about the retribution due us? Where does suffering, and punishment, and Hell fit in? I mean, I know I've done some pretty low things in my life—everyone has. So, shouldn't I be treated to at least some measure of Hell? And then, that same old cause and effect? That's still there, right? That old baggage? I mean, that's one of the Rules, isn't it?"

"Oh, there you go philosophical again. Take a break, Normie."

He raised his brows at that last expression.

"Who says there has to be Hell?" Margaret drawled. "Who says we have to simmer in agony for something that we did ever so long ago?"

"Cause and Effect says."

"No, Simon Says!" she laughed and squealed again, and then jumped up and down and sideways to make the Ferris Wheel chair rock back and forth. "Simon Says it doesn't matter!"

"It does to me," he retorted. "I want to know. Maybe Heaven is Cause and Hell is Effect? The eternal binary sequence? The swinging pendulum? The life and death cycle? Good and Evil? Male and Female?"

"Bull and Shit?"

"Don't you want to understand in the least what is happening? All our lives we've had no proof, no idea of what it's like *after* and here we are, and you don't care! Instead of answers I find more things to file away under 'real,' which results in a further re-shuffling of my mindset, which of course brings up more questions!"

"Then you should be proud of yourself, 'cause it sounds like you're doing exactly what God intended. Your vista is expanding and you are actively pursuing the discovery of the Meaning of Life. Simon Says."

"Margaret, you are infuriating."

"Simon, you're a fool."

"Norman," he reminded.

"Yeah, right whatever. Whoever you are, my friend."

Norman sighed, stretched his arms high overhead, and stared at the glittering lights far below. He then looked back in the direction "up" where he was so used to seeing a sky. There were no stars here, he thought. And overhead the Universe seemed to taper off into a haze of absolute blackness, the very Edge of an abyss which he could not even conceive.

"What about Astronomy? Where then, are all the trillions of stars, the spiral galaxies, the neutrinos, red dwarfs, cosmic dust, and atomic particles, and frozen chunks of matter in the vacuum of space? Is that an illusion we observe from our Earth's vantage, simply a curtain placed over our eyes to give us boundaries we can understand and make us feel safe?"

"You never cease, do you?" Margaret turned to him, looking in his eyes, with a faint smile, and he thought he saw a paradox of innocence and knowledge there.

"No, never," he said. "For—I miss the stars. And I would miss not having them ever again."

"Then, I guess that part would be Hell."

Suddenly he felt a touch on his shoulder, a touch of energy that seemed to crawl with warmth through his skin—or whatever he wrought into skin about himself—an intimacy more terrifying and yet wonderful than he ever imagined.

"Why would you think that any of this is necessarily mutually-exclusive?" Margaret asked, placing her hand on his shoulder (at which he burned). "Why not human astrophysics and this coexisting? I think that it's just a matter of perceiving energy, that's all. At some point, the lines of physical Earth space are blurred with other dimensions of awareness. I think, when all is brought down to the smallest, finest, most primal level, all is one, like an apple and a piece of rock is one, on a sub-atomic level.

"And furthermore," she went on, "taking these blurred lines even further, unicorns are quite real, although they were never observed by telescopes, or recorded with technical equipment. They, like astronomical phenomena, like anything else, *exist* by the very fact that we are talking about them."

"I wouldn't quite put it that way . . ." he retorted.

"I would. I did. Wake up, Norman. Really wake up. Look around you at last—not with eyes, but with your very *being*—and see that *everything* ever conceived or imagined or perceived, *exists*! It exists in the here and now, has existed, and will exist again, for that is what we are. Like God, the original Generator, we are creators on a smaller scale, our creations being as real as we are, only different in degree of intensity, for reality is a qualitative, not quantitative measure.

"If the *One* created us, then we in turn created the personal concepts of space and time to maintain our individuality, to separate ourselves from the rest. That is why there is no universal time—for time is a personal delimiter created by the self to compare and separate experience into comprehensible chunks. No universal space—for space is what consciously separates one self from another.

"Instead, there is only your kernel and my kernel of awareness, interacting with all the other 'awarenesses' through personal space-time barriers, and thus forming a perfectly shifting and yet constant form of contact with the *All*. And this whole network is the Universe!"

After that last exuberant statement, Margaret grew quiet. "So you see," she said, "I have thought about these things too, maybe even longer than you have."

To that, he had nothing to say.

Later that personal evening, they wandered in absolute silence and camaraderie, along the winding streets of LIFE, INC.

IN THE COUNTLESS personal days ahead, the desire had taken hold of Norman J. Jones over and over, until he was incandescent with the will to create. Norman brought into existence wonderful musical instruments, out of the very legends of the human race. He soon played them all, and then, after mastering winds and strings and percussion, he made music flow from the fabric of the air around him.

At first, he merely re-played all the tunes and sounds he had heard in his existence, to the best extent his memory would allow. Lulling himself with the harmony, from the very air he lifted orchestras, grand opera choruses, all of Woodstock combined, and every plaintive folk melody sung in the wilderness.

Then, when he reproduced Mozart and Led Zeppelin, he grew tired of the sounds he made. And Norman felt the *creative urge* take him further still, to the place where the earth itself, the wind, the photons of light, made music. And this music was but the vibration of the Ohm, the one sound of the Universe. And the reason it compelled him, Norman knew, was because it reminded him of the one thing, the long-ago-lost thing that was maybe truth, maybe trust, and maybe it was but the final Answer. . . .

But that desire too, left him, eventually.

So what is the point of this experience? he considered. *Is it the Buddhist Nirvana? Or something else? Is my goal here to lose all desire? To dissolve the self and be absorbed by the Cosmic Absolute? And if not, what then?*

But he did not know, and he continued to be driven by the urge.

After what felt like eons—or no time at all—Norman had mastered a succession of fields. He had scaled the Tibetan heights, piloted the Stealth and the space shuttle, written plays, discovered a cure for cancer (how terribly simple that had turned out to be, in reality)—and in the process discovered how to create gold out of base metals—pieced together the puzzle of Atlantis, and finally learned to speak Esperanto. And that's just to name a tiny few.

And very gradually, something else began happening to Norman that transformed the very nature of his desire, the force of it.

Not understanding what was happening to him, but at last too weary to care, Norman focused on a pair of brass keys (he had long since discovered there was no need to "check in" at the front desk, when all things were conjurable), and found his way through the winding quaint streets of LIFE. INC., to the HEAVEN AND HELL (TM) hotel. He opened the door to room H-23095, and without looking for the light switch, collapsed in the darkness.

Thus began the eternal night.

ONLY, eternity did not exist. Because, after timeless non-awareness, Norman found himself symbolically gasping for air, as if he'd been holding his breath underwater until the last instant possible, and came out of a stifling coma, back in the generic hotel room, lying on a nice bed, and staring at a concrete ceiling. That absolute emptiness had first created a flickering, an echo of consciousness in him, and then a spinning sensation, a sense of indescribable Universal vertigo. . . .

It was the most terrifying feeling he ever had. A feeling that by the very state of *stasis*, of *non-being*, of *pause*, he was literally falling away from the rest of the Universe which was not in stasis, but rather, in motion.

And that vertigo, that falling off, had made him flounder, had kicked in his natural instinct for survival, that final life-urge, so that he surfaced, gasping, back into forced existence.

Oh God . . . he realized. *There is no "death," no cessation, no extinction, no winking out of existence . . . no way to dissolve into nothing . . . no way to fall off this Train Ride, because according to the fundamental Rules of the Universe such separation it is a natural impossibility!*

Indeed, merely the attempt to "separate" the Self from All Else causes self-harm, damage, illness.

It is the basis of "Evil."

Thus, it was not desire that had brought Norman back this time, but a possibility of absolute destruction and harm far beyond the concept of death.

And here he was, existing, but empty of all but the most rudimentary life-bond with the Universe.

There was no previous urge to create, to achieve.

Rather, there was a total lack of it. No motivation. Emptiness. No will to get up and take a step. No flickering pull of nostalgia to remember his former earthly existence, to see the faces of the people that once surrounded him, and once mattered. No curiosity in regard to where Margaret was, to what this *place*, this afterlife, was.

No wonder about the meaning of life. No interest to further understand the unifying force of order that was One and that he could only call "God."

No cares or responsibilities. No purpose. No past. No present.

No Future.

No Hope.

Boredom.

Futility.

HELL.

The thought, like a sickness, finally came to him, to linger and take root.

So, this is it, he thought. *This is what I was waiting for all along. The emptiness, bordering on non-existence. There are no prospects open before me, because no matter what I would do, no matter what I may desire or achieve as a consequence of the pursued desire, in the end there will be an end to it. An eternity of pursuits, and then endings. Not Nirvana, but Hell. And then again, nothing. . . .*

But Norman was wrong. Slowly, as he allowed himself to remain thus, steeping in that sense of *nothing* that was barely on the verge of existence, other things started to creep back. Things that he would have referred to as "baggage." Things of the past. The Effect catching up with the Cause at last, after the long delay—or respite.

Lying on his nice generic bed, Norman J. Jones started to remember, in slow, insidious, fine detail, all the terrible, dark, evil, unfair, selfish, senseless, self-deluding, careless, self-destructive things that he was aware of—both the things that he did, and the things that others did, once, somewhere long ago. . . .

But this memory was not like the mental shock of Purgatory, with reeling senses afterwards. Instead it was gradual, methodical, and cold as steel. And also, *it did not go away*.

He remembered simple cruelty to the animals of the earth on which he lived. The human concept of eating of animal flesh.

He remembered all the World Wars, the Holocausts.

He remembered the futility, the everyday drudgery, the general misery that was the human condition. A vicious circle from which there appeared to be no way out, except by breaking human laws, going against one's principles, or engaging in self-delusion. Or, he reminded himself, there was one more way—that of superhuman *effort*. . . .

He remembered the simple everyday misunderstandings that arose because innocent words were carelessly spoken, which resulted in other darker words spoken with intent, and which escalated into alienation.

Individuals once intimate, now stood apart, revolted. And all because their wills, even when driven by the urge for beauty, by unique personal desire, did not pursue the one *true* desire—for whatever reason, most often ignorance.

Instead, in the process of achieving their immediate needs, the wills inevitably collided. One would stifle the other. One entity would try to overwhelm, while the other would shrink back, coiled into a ball of loneliness, fear, suffering, loss of self—all a result of being denied its own small freedom, the pursuit of its own misguided but vitally necessary expression of personal need.

Expression of desire....

And there were other, more indirect manifestations of this basic conflict of wills. Norman remembered his own obsession with sex, that subtle propensity for voyeurism, and that sadistic dominant streak that he often denied even to himself.

Self-denial. Now that was something. A whole new world of suffering, of obstacles placed in one's way. Only this time, the individual was in conflict with the self! This was the beginning of inner fracture, a dissipation of the one single-minded will, and a loss of balance.

Norman recalled all possible forms of self-denial besides the sexual—the ever-present self-hate that was the hate of his physical body and its various individual limitations, the disgust with his own habits, the proud disdain he felt at his own needs, and finally, the frustration with his immediate situation.

He remembered how, eventually, there came that half-conscious, gradual but absolute repression of some *needs* that disgusted him most, because he perceived them as expressions of weakness.

But he, like all others, was perverse. While denying himself some needs in order to maintain the illusory semblance of *control*, he allowed other urges to overwhelm him, giving free reign to addictions of all kinds.

He had taken drugs—starting with the "mild recreational" stuff, because at that point, the Roaring Twenties, such excess was "the thing to do," his family had the means, and he'd been curious. The curiosity was but yet another self-deluding cover-up of his unfulfilled needs, for he watched his uncle and father leave to have a "gay old time"—in the early turn-of-the century sense of the word that referred to socialite partying as opposed to sexuality—while he would stay behind. His mother would lock herself in her room, merciless, stiff and proper, and for all practical purposes his home became empty. So often he would stay seated in a chair downstairs, watching the encroaching twilight through a gray window, not moving from the same spot until total darkness. . . .

He had found the first pills in his father's cabinet. And from that point, his life became different.

But the drugs only served to uselessly vent and dissipate the constant primal urge in him, the will, the desire, the *passion* that sprung forth in him without end, and that had to be used according to its true purpose.

Caught in the vicious circle of fighting his own life-passion and its true expression, he resorted to stronger means, stronger drugs. And on the side, he learned to love the feel of hot comforting nicotine smoke in his lungs (the mother inside), and to drink the Prohibition alcohol so that his simmering passion, with no true way out, could be put down again and again, to sleep the illusory wasteful sleep, its resolution postponed indefinitely. . . .

His balance thrown off so far that he was lost in the ocean of his own drowning self, Norman J. Jones had become suicidal at the age of twenty-four—

although, the desire to let go and just drop off had visited him as early as he could remember....

However, in the back of his mind, lurked the conflicting desire to leave a shadow mark, leave a bright echo of the self behind, an intense, brilliant spark of memory, so that someone else would be touched, would remember his passing, would feel for him truly, deeply, even if only this once....

But—if lack of balance was a turbulent ocean, then peace and calm could restore him, restore the equilibrium.

During his earth existence, he had superficially "gotten his act together" toward the latter part of his surprisingly long life, after bouts of therapy to curb his substance dependency, after two World Wars, two divorces, and after his son, Jimmy, also became an addict.

The first wife left him. The second, Joanna, he left himself, for the simple reason that his outer rough hide, commonly known as "social adjustment," was only superficial, and he was beginning to feel the strain of putting up a front. Inside, he was still far off-balance, still turbulent and splashing off the edge of his inner brim.

For, he had never found a niche in life to call his own. No matter how many times he tried. No matter what kind of work he tried to occupy himself with, while his mother watched him with her icy immutable scrutiny that judged, for as long as she could, never letting up, until she too, had gone before him into the shadowed realm that followed life. . . .

But even after she was gone, he remembered the look of her eyes upon him. In it was the silent unwavering expectation that made him continually cringe, that evoked the guilt that rooted itself in him eventually, suppressed the life-urge, and became a part of his being.

And thus, even with Joanna, the only one who knew how to accept him, he could no longer pretend. He could not pretend for extended periods of time, before another being with whom he was intimate. He could no longer hide that deep inside, he was terribly missing one thing, would go on missing it until the end of his earthly days.

Peace and calm of the soul.

What is true peace? He thought. *Seriously, who even has it? Who in the history of human existence has ever had true peace?*

Is it death, unconsciousness? No, that could not be, because that implies absolute non-existence, while peace is a positive balanced state, a condition of being.

Also, as I see already, having "died," death does not exist in the traditional human sense, only change and transformation exists. And absolute death, or a breaking away from the rest of the Universe, is impossible.

In that case, peace must be complete fulfillment. And if so, then how is compete fulfillment to be achieved? By allowing one's personal desire the freedom to burn itself out . . . Or—

Or, it occurred to Norman then, was it actually the right thing for the desire to dwindle and die? Was that not the same state of boredom, this hopeless lack of purpose, this very Hell that he was living in now, that was one step away from non-existence?

Maybe the answer was to *transform the desire constantly*? To balance and modulate it on the up-swings and down-swings of the "need pendulum" until it became constant and focused and *true*?

Yes, it had to be, for the desire was his very individuality, the life-will! It had to be maintained!

To hell with Nirvana! thought Norman. *And I don't mean Kurt Cobain. To hell with Nirvana, the state of being, as we are used to understanding the concept of Nirvana.*

Only, what in the world was true desire—real desire, the one and only desire that he should strive for, and that would offer him a lifeline to scramble out of the Hell of futility, and toward the true Universal Goal?

It had to be, Norman suspected, something unselfish.

Selfish pursuits had no organized purpose but self-survival which was not a purpose in itself as much as a way of maintaining the ego. Selfish pursuits thus served to *delay*. They built up the ego and distanced the individual from the natural inevitable patterns of movement of the Universe.

It also had to be something simple, very generic. Something absolute, and that precluded death, interruption, or an end.

What forces in the Universe could fall in that category? What phenomena?

Thinking about it, Norman knew that the key word here was *movement*. Desire was a form of movement. So was light. Thought. Time. Space.

Life was movement.

The cycle of desire, from inception to fulfillment of each minor urge, was a form of progression, of movement from one state to another. And movement, in any sense, required energy.

All energy is regenerated. In the Universal sense, the original source of it is the force referred to as the "Absolute," or humanly nicknamed "God." Indeed, Norman recalled the words of the God-woman manifestation—the Universe itself was but variously moving energy.

It was the direction of movement that mattered. For, to be Universal, there had to be only one direction. The true one.

Union.

All bits of energy were innately programmed to find their own kind—to rush to join with the rest, even if they were blasted forth into opposite directions by the very act of Creation. That was the one natural universal tendency.

To return home.

The other undeniable natural universal tendency was observed in the magnet. Attraction and repulsion of positive and negative polarities. Two positive repelled, just as two negatives. A positive and a negative resulted in union.

How to reconcile these two tendencies, a tendency for indiscriminate union of incompatible bits randomly thrown together, and a tendency for complementary union?

Or maybe, there was no need to reconcile at all. Maybe, Norman thought, indiscriminate union was never the end Goal, but was merely the result of the expanding Universe, of the jigsaw broken up into little pieces, and the pieces floundering in their attempts to join again, not finding their matching neighbor pieces (those "soul mates" who were probably caught in the same dilemma somewhere on the other side of the Universe), and as a result suffering the futility of purposeless, strife-filled existence called Hell.

In the end it all came down to Humpty Dumpty. And some goddamn magnet!

This is absurd! Why am I thinking this? How did I ever get myself in so deep that I despair to the point of non-existence?

Cause and Effect, Margaret had said, does not matter. Maybe she was right after all. It's not that it does not matter—for it does. It's simply that I need not worry about it, need not think of any retribution due— simply take it when it comes!

For the very Rules of the Universe allow me that much freedom from the past, from the Effect trying to catch up. I need not bear the guilt with me, need not be my own judge, nor internalize the unfair harsh judgment of others who can never know what I know, never stand where I stand. . . . Simply hold on to the life spark of my own will, and proceed the best I can.

It is the guilt of the past that creates the weight around my spirit.

And this weight I wear on me all my days, like a dirty mud-soaked raincoat. It is this weight of guilt that makes me turn on myself and use the frustrated energy of my free will to hate my own poor being. Just as anyone would come to hate the soaked raincoat that is only getting dirtier and heavier, and requires more energy to bear—and would eventually come to associate the raincoat with the poor chilled body burdened underneath the coat.

Instead, I should be using my free will, my individuality, my desire, to move in the direction that my truth-instinct leads me.

And this appears to be my time to do just that! My personal time to cleanse and re-boot and start again. . . .

Human death, I see now, is also a personal delimiter. It brings a clean break with the immediate chronological past, and thus, a chance to forget the baggage, to take off the dirty raincoat, and to warm the spirit-body back to the heat of the true life-passion.

Death—not an ending, but an interruption.

Blessed guilt-killer.

The remover of the self-burden.

The catalyst that jump-starts each pulse in the on-going photon-stream of life.

But death had to come in its own time. Like the life urge, when the rules of the Universe kicked in, it would take place as intended, at the exact precise moment when the interruption was due.

Suicide was thus unnecessary and in fact detrimental to the flow of the cycle.

For, if the life-span was interrupted prematurely, it would have to be in some way re-played. . . . Just as a fruit had to ripen on the vine for just so long—or else, it was still green and sour, and still had to be put aside for several days to ripen the best it can, away from the vine.

There was no avoiding it, it occurred to Norman. As simple as that. And this too, only served to delay. . . .

And as he thought it, there came a sudden and absolute sense of lightness, a flash of energy.

A quickening.

He was as yet, *unfulfilled*. And yet. . . .

And yet, he knew exactly why. And he knew exactly what could make him whole.

All along he had been alone. Had been *making himself alone*.

Norman had been pursuing his desires, all the great multitudes of them, now that he could, now that he was free of the confinement of earthly life. But all the meanwhile, he was keeping himself locked away into a perspective of the self, a closed-off self-contained ego-universe.

His room, in fact—the *place* where he spent much of his personal *time*—served to emphasize the isolation, the individuality that he had surrounded himself with, the solid concrete matter, composed of great passionate creativity, within the confines of personal time and personal space.

The truth of the matter was, *his room had no walls*. It never had. Indeed, there had been no room at all.

When Norman J. Jones had been handed the pair of brass keys to room H-23095, 7th floor of HEAVEN AND HELL (TM) by the Honorable Peter, he had simply been handed an *excuse*.

It was an excuse to maintain whatever semblance of material distance that he had gotten used to during his earthly life.

Sometimes it was exciting and new, bursting with exuberance born of his eternal fountain of desire—for his desires were given the proper freedom at last. At other times, it was memories, old memories of the past that weighed down and drowned him with futile despair—for, these memories, coupled with his former mindset full of self-guilt, were what had created his own worst Hell.

Hell—even if it contains flashes of hope and brightness—is always the past, since old, once-lived sweetness can be painful also, if dwelled upon too long, and turned into nostalgia.

And Heaven is always what lies ahead of me—for,

Heaven is the hope, the life-spark, the eternal creative urge onward. And both of these states of being, I carry with me.

And what of peace?

Peace is the single clear instant of understanding all this.

The "now."

And then it's gone.

Until the next time.

Norman J. Jones thought these things, all the meanwhile growing lighter and lighter, second by personal second.

Until, there came a flash as bright as the Universe, and the last material facade-obstacle between himself and the Universe collapsed—the facade that he had personally erected and maintained around himself, perceiving it as the quaint *non-place* called "LIFE, INC."

And it was at that point that he ceased being alone, at last.

"WELL, IT CERTAINLY TOOK YOU A WHILE..." Margaret's voice sounded. Actually, it wasn't really a voice he heard—for he now had no means of auditory perception.

Instead, it was awareness of the *presence* of a

being that he had gotten to know as Margaret. She was not speaking to him in the human sense, but he had understood her *reaching out* just the same.

Just as he realized that next to her, or maybe simply all around him, there were also many *others*.

With a shock of a second Purgatory, Norman began to recognize these others, to sense them, like a smattering of stars against the black velvet of the Cosmos.

There was his grandmother Maryann Jones, smiling at him. She, who'd died when he was four, just when he had gotten to love the smell of her warm old hair, like wheat husk and sun, and antique Victorian violets, while she rocked him against her breast. . . .

And there was uncle William who had been young and debonair, and grinned with flashing white teeth. Somewhat older, but still debonair, he'd died during the Second World War, and they had brought his mangled body to be buried beneath a flag, for he had been a hero.

His second wife, Joanna, was there, young as he had remembered her last, but with shining eyes. . . .

His father, with the rare true smile. Always charming, always distant, and even now, somewhat aloof, remote, and yet—

His mother.

The *presence* that he had recognized last, had also been the same presence that he had known first.

Proud. Impeccable. A rock.

Judgment and silence.

She was the one. The one, long, long ago, who had surrounded him, a single infant spark, enveloped him with her momentarily warm *self*, her one and only moment of welcome—for he had remembered diving into a tunnel, a tornado, the eye of the storm, somewhere, sometime long, long ago. . . .

Forgive me . . . she seemed to say. *I did the best I could. For I too, had been lost . . . Alone. Forgive me, I did not know any better. I did not know how to love you enough . . . How to love . . . I did not know. . . .*

And the presences—not people, but evoking still the familiar physical images in him—converged upon him, and encircled him with vibrant welcome. And he knew them for what they were—stars, bright bits of auric energy, pulsing like torn fragments of a single rainbow. Uniform, and yet unique.

Lights.

He too was a light.

Norman J. Jones felt the bottom falling out from under him, for he saw himself true at last, without a body, without the five senses. Only light. . . .

He sensed himself spanning all across the Universe, his being of energy merging with the bright network of other clusters of energy, other lights. . . . And with it came a pulsing warmth, a sensation of blending in, and finally, perfect balance.

Welcome! came from the presence that he knew as Margaret. *You have cleansed yourself of the grime of a lifetime. You are now free. And you are ready to continue with the next cycle.*

*But how—*he began.

Follow me! Margaret cried. And he saw superimposed, images of a child, an old woman, and a young woman with burning red hair.

Who are you? he echoed.

Cosmic laughter was his answer, bubbling with joy like the spring of his own desires.

Why, Norman, you silly, silly love! Who do you think I am? I am still the same that I was before. The only difference is, now I know you, and you know me. While before, we didn't.

We were two sparks never previously thrown together. We are now given a chance to mingle and see what resulting new wonder comes about.

The Margaret-presence neared him, and he felt a light touch of warmth, which then gained in intensity, becoming hot, then incandescent, so that he burned. But the hot brightness was ecstasy, a merging of fire with fire. And a perfect contentment followed.

My new love . . . came her whisper. *I must go before you this once. Soon after, you too will follow. You will know when, for it will be but a second in your personal time-frame. I, however, will make ready for you, to receive you. . . . You will be very different, and I will be a little different. And yet, both of us in essence will be the same.*

And as she said this, she, the light-form, broke away from him (so that with a pang he immediately missed the warmth, the fire of her). As she left him, he felt for an instant only, a renewal of that terrifying fear, that sense of being torn off from the rest of the Universe.

But that was for an instant only.

For, his life-urge, the passion, was burning steady and balanced and bright—precisely as he himself was bright. And with it, he had hope to hold on to, a Heaven of things to come.

Having known the re-affirmation of *union*, there could now be no fear. Instead, there was a faint germination, a renewal of innocence. With tender shoots, the seed of trust had once again taken root in his being.

Innocence is not the same as naïveté, he considered. *Naïveté is the first stage, the lack of awareness, before experience. Experience is the second stage, after which comes disillusionment, or renewal. That renewal is what constitutes true innocence.*

Innocence is the persistence of trust even after experience comes crashing down on you and challenges your sense of hope and your connection with universal truth—challenges your one and only sure bond with the Universe.

Innocence is thus the third stage, when trust is equipped with the knowledge of the world, of its rules and limits, of what is possible and what is not, and is thus strong enough to withstand anything.

Thus, all are born naive. All gain experience. Most are broken by it, and have to forget, before they can start again. But the remaining few are forged by the experience to be cynical, and then, truly innocent, holding on to trust and truth, simply because they now can. It is only then that death, the delimiter, becomes unnecessary, and all knowledge of the past is retained, together with the simultaneous awareness of the future.

But—that is still far ahead. . . . Somewhere, far ahead, lies that particular Heaven. . . .

I am only as imperfect as I allow myself to be, he thought. *But for the moment, that is what I am, and there is no guilt in it.*

Because someday, I will be otherwise. And I will know all truth.

And in that instant, Norman J. Jones felt a pull, a great force calling him—fierce with passion, a maelstrom.

And pulled by that instinctive call, a primeval urge that was simply love, he, the entity once called Norman J. Jones, was torn, twisted, thrust, and *she* was now falling, falling, falling . . .

. . . with a hoarse cry tearing young, fierce lungs, gasping her first breath of oxygen, she was struggling to surface, pulled and supported by large, strong hands.

The infant girl made her way out of the warm, safe oblivion-darkness of the birth canal, and was greeted with exuberant, vaguely focused faces of those that would be her loved ones.

Upside down, the child was lifted, while the world tilted on a crazy angle that she could not yet distinguish or perceive, but soon would.

Below her, on the birthing table, lay a thirtyish woman with sweat-drenched red hair like sunset fire. A smile holding in it all possible cosmic truth was on her face, as she reached out with eager hands for the newborn. The energy in her eyes was that of a thirteen-year-old, while the expression contained there was simple, unconditional, ageless true love.

AFTERWORD

If you enjoyed reading this philosophical fable, try the inspirational daily diary / journal / workbook:

THE PERPETUAL CALENDAR OF INSPIRATION:
Old Wisdom for a New World

366 Days of Insight from the Inspired.Us Blog

by the same author.

For more information and inspirational entires, visit:
inspiredus.com

Or buy at a wide variety of bookstores online:
https://books2read.com/b/ml5vxZ

DON'T MISS ANOTHER BOOK BY VERA NAZARIAN!

Subscribe to the mailing list to be notified when the next books by Vera Nazarian are available:

veranazarian.com/signup.html

We promise not to spam you or chit-chat, only make occasional book release and news announcements.

OTHER BOOKS BY VERA NAZARIAN

Lords of Rainbow

Dreams of the Compass Rose

Salt of the Air

The Perpetual Calendar of Inspiration

The Clock King and the Queen of the Hourglass

Mayhem at Grant-Williams High (YA)

The Duke in His Castle

After the Sundial

Supernatural Jane Austen Series:
Mansfield Park and Mummies

Northanger Abbey and Angels and Dragons

Pride and Platypus: Mr. Darcy's Dreadful Secret

Vampires are from Venus, Werewolves are from Mars:
A Comprehensive Guide to Attracting Supernatural Love

Cobweb Bride Trilogy:
Cobweb Bride

Cobweb Empire

Cobweb Forest

The Atlantis Grail:

Qualify (Book One)

Compete (Book Two)

Win (Book Three)

Survive (Book Four)

The Atlantis Grail Novella Series

Aeson: Blue

Aeson: Black

The Atlantis Grail Superfan Extras

The Atlantis Grail Companion

People of the Atlantis Grail

(Forthcoming)

Dawn of the Atlantis Grail (TAG Prequel Series)

Eos (Book One)

Dea (Book Two)

Niktos (Book Three)

Ghost (Book Four)

Starlight (Book Five)

The Atlantis Grail:

The Book of Everything (Book Five)

The Atlantis Grail Novella Series

Xelio: Red

Brie: Red

Thank you for your support!

ABOUT THE AUTHOR

Vera Nazarian is a two-time Nebula Award® Finalist, a Dragon Award 2018 Finalist, and a member of Science Fiction and Fantasy Writers Association. As a double refugee, after immigrating from the USSR during the Cold War, and then escaping from the Civil War in Lebanon (by way of Greece), she spent 35 years in Los Angeles, California. She sold her first story at 17, and has been published in numerous anthologies and magazines, honorably mentioned in Year's Best volumes, and translated into eight languages.

Vera made her novelist debut with the critically acclaimed *Dreams of the Compass Rose* (2002), followed by *Lords of Rainbow* (2003). Her novella *The Clock King and the Queen of the Hourglass* made the 2005 Locus Recommended Reading List. Her debut collection *Salt of the Air* contains the 2007 Nebula Award-nominated "The Story of Love." Other work includes the 2008 Nebula Finalist novella *The Duke in His Castle*, science fiction collection *After the Sundial* (2010), *The*

Perpetual Calendar of Inspiration (2010), three Jane Austen parodies, *Mansfield Park and Mummies* (2009), *Northanger Abbey and Angels and Dragons* (2010), and *Pride and Platypus: Mr. Darcy's Dreadful Secret* (2012), all part of her *Supernatural Jane Austen Series*, a parody of self-help and supernatural relationships advice, *Vampires are from Venus, Werewolves are from Mars: A Comprehensive Guide to Attracting Supernatural Love* (2012), *Cobweb Bride Trilogy* (2013), the bestselling international cross-genre phenomenon series *The Atlantis Grail*, now optioned for development as a feature film and/or TV series, *Qualify* (2014), *Compete* (2015), *Win* (2017), and *Survive* (2020), the novellas *Aeson: Blue* (2021), Aeson: Black (2022), fan reference guides *The Atlantis Grail Companion* (2021), and *People of the Atlantis Grail* (2023).

After many years in Los Angeles, Vera now lives with multiple wacky cats in a small town in Vermont. She uses her Armenian sense of humor and her Russian sense of suffering to bake conflicted pirozhki and make art.

In addition to being a writer, philosopher, and award-winning artist, she is also the publisher of Norilana Books.

Official website: https://www.veranazarian.com

Get on my Mailing List! https://www.veranazarian.com/signup.html

The Atlantis Grail Fan Discussion Forum:

https://atlantisgrail.proboards.com/

Astra Daimon and Shoelace Girls (Facebook fan group):

https://www.facebook.com/groups/adasg/

The Atlantis Grail – SPOILERS (Facebook fan group):

https://www.facebook.com/groups/tag2spoilers

TAG official website: https://www.theatlantisgrail.com/

TAG Fandom website: https://www.tag.fan

Norilana Books: https://www.norilana.com/

Twitter: https://twitter.com/Norilana

Facebook: https://www.facebook.com/VeraNazarian

TikTok: https://www.tiktok.com/@veranazarian

Instagram: https://www.instagram.com/vera_nazarian/

YouTube Channel: https://www.youtube.com/veranazarian-tag

Scan Code for Linktree.

www.ingramcontent.com/pod-product-compliance
Lightning Source LLC
Chambersburg PA
CBHW022122040426
42450CB00006B/802